THE ABC's of BLACK HISTORY

WRITTEN BY DELORIS L. HOLT • ILLUSTRATED BY SAMUEL BHANG, JR.

THE WARD RITCHIE PRESS • LOS ANGELES

FOR CHESTER
AND IN MEMORY OF PEARL AND WILLIS ADAMS

2nd Printing, 1973

Copyright © 1971 by Deloris L. Holt
Printed in the United States of America
Designed by Samuel Bhang, Jr. and Joseph Simon
Library of Congress Catalog Card Number 70-142550
ISBN 0378-61043-0

IT IS MY SINCERE HOPE THAT THIS BOOK WILL SERVE A DUAL PURPOSE. FIRST, AS AN INTRODUCTION FOR BLACK BOYS AND GIRLS TO OUR OWN HISTORY; AND THEN, FOR ALL BOYS AND GIRLS, A BRIEF GUIDE TO A FEW OF THE MANY CONTRIBUTIONS BLACK AMERICANS HAVE MADE TO THIS COUNTRY / **DELORIS L. HOLT**

IRA ALDRIDGE
1807-1867

Ira Aldridge was born near Baltimore, Maryland. He was the son of an African chieftain. His father was brought by missionaries from Senegal to the United States, and he later became a minister. Ira attended the African Free School in New York City.

Ira's father wanted him to study medicine, but Ira wanted to become an actor. When he was about seventeen his father sent him to Scotland to study at the University of Glasgow. But Ira could not forget his love of the theater. He soon left school and went to London to appear on the stage.

Ira was a great success as an actor. He became a star in London's most famous theater. Soon he was one of the greatest actors in all of Europe. He appeared in Berlin, Amsterdam, Vienna and all the major cities. He was awarded medals by the King of Prussia, the King of Sweden, and the Emperor of Russia.

Ira Aldridge was so great an actor that people watching him perform would forget that he was acting. Once in a scene that required him to stab an actress, a man ran from the audience begging him not to kill her because she was innocent. The man was so carried away by Ira's performance that he thought Ira was really going to kill the actress.

Ira Aldridge left his country because he knew that a black man could not perform on the stage in America. He never performed in his own country. He died in Poland in 1867.

BENJAMIN BANNEKER
1731-1806

Benjamin Banneker was born free during the time when most black people were slaves. His mother was a free woman and his father was a slave.

Benjamin's grandmother, who was an Englishwoman, taught him to read. He showed such a talent for mathematics and science that a wealthy white neighbor, George Ellicott, willingly supplied him with books. Benjamin read and studied all the books he could get. He educated himself and became one of the most gifted astronomers and mathematicians of his time.

When he was a young man, Benjamin built the first clock to be made in America. The clock kept accurate time until he died.

Benjamin was also an expert surveyor. He could measure and lay out land for towns and cities. He was chosen by Thomas Jefferson to help lay out the site of the new capital. Benjamin worked with a Frenchman, Pierre L'Enfant, in surveying the land for the new capital. In 1792 L'Enfant was dismissed from the surveying team because of an argument with George Washington. He returned to France and took all the plans for the new capital with him.

Benjamin Banneker was able to reproduce the plans from memory and thus made the construction of Washington D. C. possible.

GEORGE WASHINGTON CARVER
1864-1943

Dr. George Washington Carver was born a slave in Diamond Grove, Missouri. By the time he was thirteen years old he was taking care of himself. He wanted to get an education. Dr. Carver worked his way through Simpson and Iowa State Colleges.

Dr. Carver became a famous botanist. He was interested in helping the southern states find more crops to raise. Most southern farmers depended on one crop, cotton. Whenever there was not a good cotton crop the farmers made very little money. Dr. Carver knew that it would help the farmers if they could raise other things. He showed them that by growing peanuts, sweet potatoes, and soybeans they could have more than one crop to sell.

Dr. Carver made many things from these new crops. From the peanut he made meal, instant coffee, bleach, paper, ink, shaving cream, plastic and metal polish. He made flour, breakfast food and milk from the soybean; and he made more than one hundred products from the sweet potato.

Dr. Carver received many honors for his work. Scientists from all over the world came to talk and study with him. He received the Roosevelt Medal for his services to science in 1939.

George Washington Carver was the genius who gave us so many things that we take for granted today.

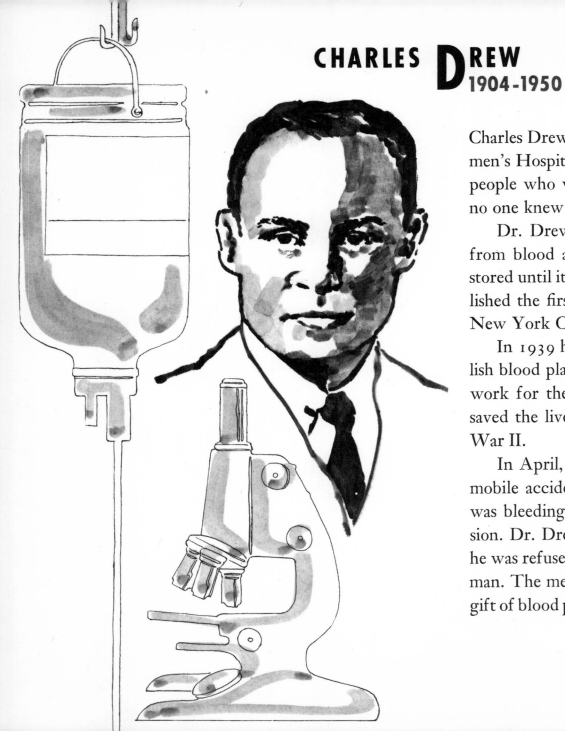

CHARLES DREW
1904-1950

Charles Drew was a doctor. He was the head of Freedmen's Hospital in Washington D.C. Before Dr. Drew, people who were sick and needed blood died because no one knew how to store and save blood.

Dr. Drew discovered the way to separate plasma from blood and store it. The blood plasma could be stored until it was needed to save a life. Dr. Drew established the first blood bank at Presbyterian Hospital in New York City.

In 1939 he was asked to come to England to establish blood plasma banks there. In 1942 he did the same work for the United States. His blood plasma banks saved the lives of thousands of soldiers during World War II.

In April, 1950, Dr. Drew was injured in an automobile accident near Burlington, North Carolina. He was bleeding very badly and needed a blood transfusion. Dr. Drew was taken to the nearest hospital, but he was refused medical attention because he was a black man. The medical genius who had given the world the gift of blood plasma died because it was not given to him.

EDWARD KENNEDY (DUKE) ELLINGTON
1899-

Edward Kennedy Ellington began taking piano lessons when he was seven years old. He would practice his piano lessons, but he liked making up his own melodies better. He wrote his first song when he was seventeen years old.

Edward enjoyed sports and art also. He thought he might become a commercial artist. His first job was in an ice cream parlor. There was a piano and sometimes, when he was not busy, he would play for the customers. He decided to become a musician.

Edward loved nice clothes and was always dressed neatly. His friends started calling him "Duke" because of the way he dressed. The name stayed with him the rest of his life.

Duke Ellington has become one of America's most famous composers. His orchestra has played all over the world. He has written over one thousand songs. His "Black, Brown, and Beige Suite" is a musical history of black people in America.

Duke Ellington received the Presidential Award in 1969 for his achievements. President Richard Nixon gave a birthday party for him in the White House to celebrate his 70th birthday. People came from all over the country to his party. They came to honor one of America's great musicians.

HENRY OSSIAN FLIPPER
1856-1940

Henry Flipper was nine years old when freedom came to the slaves. He wanted to go to school so that he could become educated. Henry's family moved to the city so that he could go to a school for the newly freed slaves.

Henry received an appointment to go to the United States Military Academy at West Point. He was the first black man to go to West Point. Henry studied very hard and was a good student even though the other students at West Point treated him very badly.

Henry graduated in 1877 and was the only graduate to receive cheers during the graduation program. Henry deserved the cheers because his life at West Point had been very hard.

Henry Flipper became the first black officer in the 10th Cavalry. The 10th Cavalry was an all black unit of soldiers who fought the Indians. They were called the Buffalo Soldiers.

After serving in the army, Henry became a mining engineer. He worked in Mexico and Venezuela. Henry Flipper served his own country further by becoming an advisor to the Secretary of the Interior. He died in 1940.

DEBORAH SAMPSON GANNETT

Deborah Sampson Gannett was a black woman who lived in the colony of Massachusetts. She was the first woman to serve in the army in this country.

Deborah loved freedom. When the Revolutionary War began, she wanted to help fight for our country's freedom. But Deborah knew that women could not join the army.

On May 20, 1782, she dressed herself to look like a man and joined the 4th Massachusetts Regiment as a regular soldier. She used the name of Robert Shurtliff to join the army. Deborah was a good soldier. She served in the army for almost a year before she was discovered to be a woman. After she was discovered she had to leave the army.

Deborah Gannett fought so well that her state praised her for her bravery and awarded her a cash bonus for her service to our country.

MATTHEW ALEXANDER HENSON
1866-1955

Matthew Henson loved adventure. He liked to go to far away places and see and do new things. Matthew visited China, Asia, Africa, Europe and the South Pacific Islands.

When Matthew heard that some men were going to try to reach the North Pole, he wanted to go too. Matthew knew that this would be the greatest adventure of his life.

The men who were trying to reach the North Pole were led by Admiral Robert E. Peary. They suffered many hardships. The cold was terrible; some suffered from snowblindness, and some became ill. Finally, on April 6, 1909, Matthew was the only one able to go on with the expedition. He was the first man to reach the North Pole where he placed an American flag.

Matthew Alexander Henson was awarded the civil Congressional Medal of Honor for his achievement.

BOSE IKARD
1847-1929

Bose Ikard was born a slave in Mississippi. When he was a little boy, his owner moved his family and all of his slaves to Texas. Texas was still the frontier and everyone had to work very hard building their homes. Bose learned to ride horses and rope and catch cattle. He learned to fight for what he thought was right.

After the Civil War, when the slaves were freed, Bose went to work for a man named Charles Goodnight. He would work the cattle drives because he was an expert rider and roper.

Bose and Charles Goodnight became good friends. Bose saved Charles' life several times. Whenever they sold the cattle Bose carried the money because no one dared try to rob him. He was always cool and kept his head no matter what was happening. During a cattle stampede or an Indian raid, Bose was right up front leading the men.

Bose Ikard was a Texas pioneer. He lived and worked in Texas the rest of his life.

SAUNDERS JACKSON

Saunders Jackson was a black man who helped explore and map the way from Wyoming to California. The expedition to find a new way to California was led by Captain John C. Fremont.

Saunders volunteered to go because he wanted to earn seventeen hundred dollars to buy his family out of slavery.

The men were trying to find a pass through the Rocky Mountains so that a railroad to California could be built. They became lost in the mountains and had to turn back. A blinding snowstorm buried them. Many of the men died.

Saunders and Captain Fremont tried a southern way and finally reached California in 1849. When they arrived they found that gold had been discovered.

Saunders Jackson began to dig for gold for he still wanted to buy his family's freedom. He dug seventeen hundred dollars worth of gold from the ground in just a few days. With this money he returned to Missouri where his family were slaves and bought their freedom.

Saunders Jackson moved his family away from Missouri and no one ever heard of him again.

MARTIN LUTHER KING
1929-1968

Martin Luther King loved everyone. He preached that love and brotherhood were needed by all Americans. He taught that violence was not the way for black people to gain their rights.

Martin wanted all people to have the same rights. In the town where he lived, black people had to ride in the back of the bus. The Montgomery, Alabama bus company also said that black people had to get up and give their seats to white people when the bus became crowded.

One day a black woman, Mrs. Rosa Parks, would not get up and give her seat to a white man. Mrs. Parks was tired because she had worked all day and she wanted to sit down while she rode the bus home. Mrs. Parks was arrested because she would not give up her seat. Martin knew that it was wrong for Mrs. Parks to be in jail. He helped to organize all the black people in Montgomery. Martin told them not to ride the buses anymore until they could sit down anywhere on the bus.

The people did not ride the buses for 381 days. They formed car pools; drivers would take turns driving people to and from places instead of using buses. Many people walked long distances to work and home again because they knew they were helping in the fight. Finally the bus company had to give in to the demands of the people. They had lost so much money because no one was riding the buses that they were ready to go out of business. The people had won their battle.

In 1968 Martin was in Memphis, Tennessee, trying to help black city workers get better pay. He was shot as he stood on a porch talking to some friends. Martin Luther King died from an assassin's bullet on April 4, 1968.

LOUIS HOWARD LATIMER
1848-1928

Louis Latimer helped to bring us light. After Thomas Edison invented the electric light bulb, Louis worked to improve it.

He made a thin metal wire called a filament, and placed it inside the bulb: this caused the bulb to give better light. Louis also improved the socket of the bulb. The metal socket we use today is just like the wooden socket made by Louis Latimer.

Louis worked with Alexander Graham Bell. He helped to make the patent drawings for the first telephone. He was the chief draftsman for General Electric and Westinghouse Companies. Louis supervised the installation of electric light in New York City, Philadelphia, Montreal, Canada, and London, England.

Louis Howard Latimer was a member of the Edison Pioneers. He was one of the creators of the electric light.

DORIE MILLER
1919-1943

Dorie Miller was a sailor on the battleship Arizona. He was a mess-man; a waiter who served food. At that time, black men were only allowed to do cooking and serving jobs in the navy. But Dorie was proud to be a sailor in the United States Navy.

During the attack on Pearl Harbor in 1941, Dorie was finally able to fight. He carried the wounded captain of his ship to safety. He then took the gun of a sailor who had also been wounded; and although he had never fired the gun before, he shot down four Japanese planes.

Dorie became one of the first heroes of World War II. He was awarded the Navy Cross for his bravery. He was killed on Thanksgiving Day, 1943, when his ship, the Liscome Bay, was torpedoed and sunk.

PEDRO ALONSO NINO

Pedro Alonso Niño was a black man who was with Columbus when he discovered the New World. There were three ships; the Niña, the Pinta, and the Santa Maria. Columbus sailed on the Santa Maria and Pedro guided the Niña across the ocean.

Pedro and the other sailors suffered many hardships in crossing the ocean on their little ships. There was little food and drinking water. Many of the sailors wanted to turn back for home. They were afraid. Pedro believed in Columbus. He knew that they would find land.

One morning they saw land birds flying over their ships and a sailor saw branches and flowers floating in the water. They knew that this meant land was near. Finally on Friday, October 12, 1492, they saw land.

Pedro Alonso Niño came ashore with Columbus. They fell to their knees to thank God for bringing them safely across the ocean. Pedro and the other men with Columbus stayed in the New World for several weeks. During their stay Columbus's ship, the Santa Maria, was destroyed by a storm. It was Pedro's ship, the Niña, that carried Columbus back to Spain to tell the news of the New World.

JESSE OWENS
1913-

Jesse Owens went to Berlin, Germany in 1936 as part of the United States Olympic Team.

Jesse was proud to represent his country. He knew that Adolph Hitler, the leader of Germany, had said that black men were not as good as white men. Hitler thought that the German team was the best and would win all the medals.

Jesse proved that the Germans were not the best athletes. He won the 100-meter dash, the 200-meter dash and the broad jump. He ran on the relay team and the team won.

Jesse's victories upset Hitler so much that he refused to stay to see the medals awarded to the winners.

The "Star Spangled Banner" was played each time an American received a medal. Jesse Owens stood with pride as it played. He received three gold medals and made all of America proud of him.

BILL PICKETT
1840(?)-1932

Bill Pickett was one of the West's most famous cowboys. Bill worked on a large ranch in Oklahoma called the 101 Ranch. He worked with many other cowboys; among them were Tom Mix and Will Rogers.

Bill created the art of bulldogging or steer wrestling. Bill would ride his horse along side a running bull and then jump off onto the bull. He would wrestle the steer to the ground by holding it by the horns. Sometimes Bill would bring the bull to the ground with just his teeth. He would jump from his horse and grab the steer's lip and let go with his hands. This would bring the bull to the ground.

Bill rode and performed in shows in Chicago, New York City, London and Mexico City. He was always the most exciting part of the show.

Bulldogging is still part of rodeos today. But the cowboys do not use their teeth to bring down the steers. Only Bill Pickett could do that.

BENJAMIN QUARLES
1904-

Benjamin Quarles is a writer and teacher. Benjamin wanted everyone to know about the brave deeds that black people have performed in our country's wars. He has written books about the Revolutionary War and the Civil War. Benjamin knew that it was important for everyone to know that black people helped to fight in both wars.

Benjamin also wrote books about Frederick Douglass and Abraham Lincoln, two famous men who lived during the time of the Civil War.

Benjamin Quarles teaches history at Morgan State College in Baltimore, Maryland.

NORBERT RILLIEUX
1806-1894

Norbert Rillieux was born a slave. His father was master of a plantation and his mother was a slave on the plantation. Norbert's father sent him to Paris to be educated. He became an engineer and taught at L'Ecole Centrale in France. When he returned to New Orleans, he was given his freedom.

Norbert was interested in the way sugar was made. He wanted to find a cheaper way to make it. The process of making sugar was so expensive that it made the cost very high. Only rich people could buy it. Poor people could not afford sugar so they used molasses or honey instead.

Norbert invented a vacuum pan and vacuum chamber that completely changed the way sugar was made. The sugar producers of Louisiana would not use the new method that Norbert had invented. Norbert became very discouraged and decided to return to France. He tried to interest the sugar producers of Europe in his new process.

After ten years, some European sugar producers who owned plantations in the West Indies began using Norbert's process. Norbert began improving his invention and finally the American sugar producers began to use it also.

Norbert Rillieux made it possible for everyone to use sugar. The largest sugar manufacturers in the United States have placed a bronze tablet in the state museum of Louisiana in honor of this great man.

ROBERT SMALLS
1839-1915

Robert Smalls was a slave who was forced to work on a southern ship at the beginning of the Civil War. Robert decided to steal the ship and escape from slavery to the north. He waited until the captain and crew had gone ashore, then he secretly brought his wife and two children aboard.

Robert knew they would be killed if they were caught, but he wanted to be free. The other slaves on board worked with him as Robert guided the ship through dangerous waters until he reached the Union lines. There he turned the southern ship over to the Union.

Robert was asked to stay on as pilot. During a fierce battle the captain became afraid and abandoned the ship. Robert took over and guided it out of danger. Because of his bravery, Robert was made captain of the ship for the rest of the war.

After the war Robert Smalls continued to serve his country. He was elected to the South Carolina House of Representatives and the South Carolina Senate. In 1875 he was elected to the United States House of Representatives. He served as a representative of his state in Congress until 1887.

HARRIET TUBMAN
1823-1913

Harriet Tubman was born a slave. When she was a very young woman, she ran away and made her way to freedom in the north.

Harriet became the most famous conductor for the underground railroad. The underground was not a real railroad. Brave black people who wanted to be free would escape and travel at night; stopping only at the houses of friends to rest. They knew that to be caught meant that they would be punished and sent back into slavery. The leader who guided the runaway slaves was called a conductor, and the route they traveled in secret was known as the underground railroad.

During the Civil War, Harriet served as a nurse, scout, and spy for the Union army. She led a raid against the enemy which freed hundreds of slaves and captured food and materials for the Union army.

Harriet Tubman served her country well. Although she could not read or write, she made many trips into the slave states to help her people to freedom. With only the North Star to guide her, she rescued more than 300 slaves. She proudly said, "I never run my train off the track and I never lost a passenger!"

JAMES UNDERDUE

James Underdue wanted to fight in the Civil War. He knew that the war was about freedom for the slaves, and he believed everyone should be free. But James was a minister and he did not want to kill anyone. He wanted to find another way to fight for freedom.

James knew that men going into battle needed someone to talk to. The soldiers often wanted to pray before a battle. The wounded soldiers needed someone to comfort them. So James became a chaplain. He went with the soldiers into battle. He was there to help them in any way he could.

James Underdue served with the 39th Regiment of Colored Troops. He fought for freedom in his own peaceful way.

DENMARK VESEY
1767-1822

Denmark Vesey was born in St. Thomas on the island of San Domingo. When he was about fourteen he was captured and brought to the United States as a slave. Denmark became the slave of a Captain Vesey, a ship's captain. He sailed on Captain Vesey's ship for almost twenty years and visited many places.

Denmark remembered what freedom was like when he was a boy. He visited Haiti with Captain Vesey. There he saw black men working in their own government. Denmark decided that all the slaves should be free.

In 1800 Denmark won a lottery of fifteen hundred dollars. He used the money to buy his freedom. Then he began to plan a way for the slaves of Charleston, South Carolina, to become free.

He told the slaves that they should rise up and kill all the white people in Charleston, and then take control of the city. Denmark and other slaves who joined him began to buy guns and hide them. They bought wigs, false beards and clothing for their revolt. They plotted and planned for several years. By the time Denmark thought they were ready, nine thousand slaves had joined in the plan.

Denmark was betrayed by a black man who worked as a house servant. He was caught and put into prison and sentenced to hang. An offer was made to save his life if he would confess and tell who the other leaders of the revolt were.

Denmark Vesey went to his death in 1822 rather than confess. His plan had failed but he died for freedom.

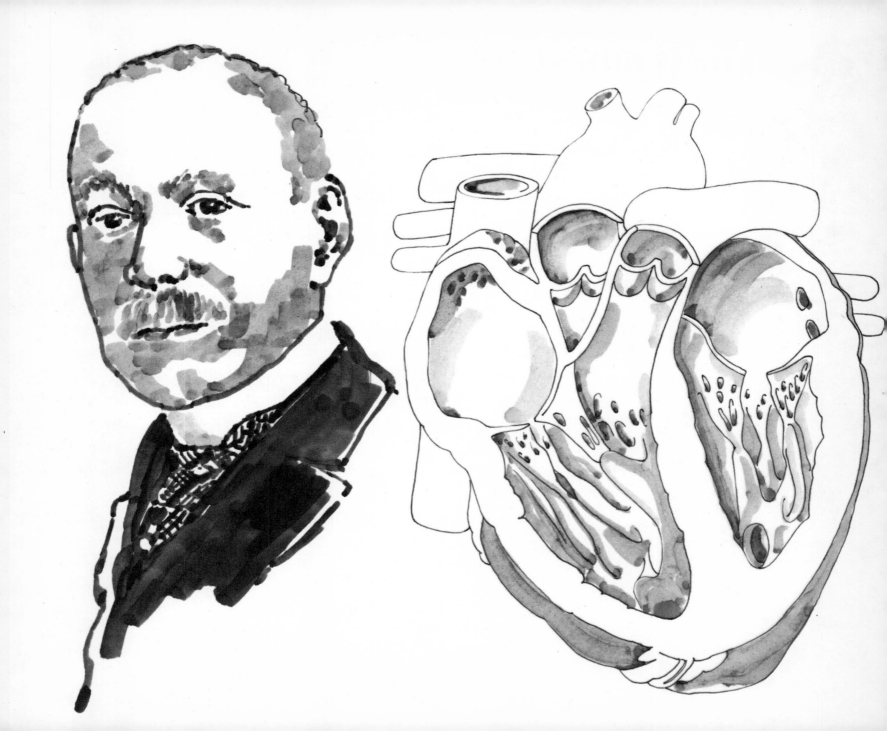

DANIEL HALE WILLIAMS
1858-1931

Daniel Hale Williams became a doctor in 1883. He was graduated from the medical school of Northwestern University in Chicago, Illinois. After graduation, he taught at Northwestern University's medical school. He was asked by the president of the United States, Grover Cleveland, to go to Washington D. C. to head the Freedmen's Hospital there. Freedmen's Hospital was one of the few hospitals for blacks in the United States.

Dr. Williams returned to Chicago to help found Provident Hospital, which was to be a place where black doctors could work. Before Provident Hospital opened, black doctors in Chicago had to treat their patients in their homes. Operations were performed on couches and kitchen tables because white hospitals would not permit black doctors to work there. Dr. Williams also helped to set up the first training school for black nurses at Provident Hospital in 1891.

Daniel Hale Williams performed the first successful operation on the human heart in 1893. A man was dying because he had been stabbed in his heart. Heart wounds had always meant death. Dr. Williams did not have X-rays or blood transfusions to help him. But he decided that he would try to save the man's life. Dr. Williams opened the man's chest and sewed up his heart. His daring operation was a success. The man lived.

Daniel Hale Williams was a medical pioneer.

MALCOLM X 1925-1965

Malcolm X was born Malcolm Little. Malcolm refused to use his last name. He said that the last names of black people were the last names of their masters when they were slaves. He changed his last name to X.

Malcolm was a great speaker. He told black people to be proud of their black skin. He told them they would succeed in getting equal rights by helping themselves, and not by depending on others to help them. Malcolm encouraged black people to save their money, to be clean, and to always be honest.

Malcolm visited many countries in Africa. He believed that black people all over the world should unite in brotherhood.

Malcolm X was shot and killed while making a speech in New York City in 1965.

CHARLES YOUNG
1864-1922

Charles Young was the third black man to graduate from West Point. He served in the army in Mexico, Cuba, Haiti, and Liberia. He was also a professor of military science at Wilberforce University in Ohio.

When the United States entered World War I, Colonel Young wanted to fight for his country. Colonel Young was the only living black West Point graduate, and the highest ranking black officer in the army. This meant that he would have become a brigadier-general and would command white troops.

The army did not want a black man commanding white troops. The army told Colonel Young that he was to retire. They said he was too old to fight and not in good health. Colonel Young was fifty three years old, and he knew that his health was fine. He decided to prove to the army that he was healthy and not too old to help fight the war. He rode his horse alone from his home in Ohio five hundred miles to Washington D. C. But it did no good, for the army still would not let him fight. He was assigned to train black troops in Fort Grant, Illinois. Later, he was sent to Liberia, in Africa, to help organize the army there.

Colonel Charles Young died of a fever in Liberia in 1922.

Henry Zino lived in New Orleans. Henry loved music. The drums were his favorite instrument. Henry learned to play the drums by himself.

At the beginning of this century, when Henry lived in New Orleans, a new kind of music called jazz was being played. Jazz was so new that no one played from sheets of music; the musicians played the music the way they felt it should sound.

The jazz bands played in many places. They played for picnics, for dances, and even for funerals. The musicians didn't make much money, only a dollar or two a night, but they didn't care because they loved music.

Henry, who was sometimes called Henry Baltimore, played in many New Orleans jazz bands. He moved to Texas and took jazz with him. Soon jazz was being played all over the country.

Henry Zino helped create a new kind of music. Jazz became the only true American form of music.

HENRY **Z**INO